HowI

MW01611655

Basketball Referee 101

101 Tips to Start, Grow, and Succeed as a Basketball Official From A to Z

HowExpert with Steven Michaluk

For more tips related to this topic, visit HowExpert.com/basketballreferee.

Recommended Resources

- HowExpert.com – Quick 'How To' Guides on All Topics from A to Z by Everyday Experts.
- HowExpert.com/free – Free HowExpert Email Newsletter.
- HowExpert.com/books – HowExpert Books
- HowExpert.com/courses – HowExpert Courses
- HowExpert.com/clothing – HowExpert Clothing
- HowExpert.com/membership – HowExpert Membership Site
- HowExpert.com/affiliates – HowExpert Affiliate Program
- HowExpert.com/writers – Write About Your #1 Passion/Knowledge/Expertise & Become a HowExpert Author.
- HowExpert.com/resources – Additional HowExpert Recommended Resources
- YouTube.com/HowExpert – Subscribe to HowExpert YouTube.
- Instagram.com/HowExpert – Follow HowExpert on Instagram.
- Facebook.com/HowExpert – Follow HowExpert on Facebook.

Publisher's Foreword

Dear HowExpert reader,

HowExpert publishes quick 'how to' guides on all topics from A to Z by everyday experts.

At HowExpert, our mission is to discover, empower, and maximize talents of everyday people to ultimately make a positive impact in the world for all topics from A to Z...one everyday expert at a time!

All of our HowExpert guides are written by everyday people just like you and me who have a passion, knowledge, and expertise for a specific topic.

We take great pride in selecting everyday experts who have a passion, great writing skills, and knowledge about a topic that they love to be able to teach you about the topic you are also passionate about and eager to learn about.

We hope you get a lot of value from our HowExpert guides and it can make a positive impact in your life in some kind of way. All of our readers including you altogether help us continue living our mission of making a positive impact in the world for all spheres of influences from A to Z.

If you enjoyed one of our HowExpert guides, then please take a moment to send us your feedback from wherever you got this book.

Thank you and we wish you all the best in all aspects of life.

Sincerely,

BJ Min
Founder & Publisher of HowExpert
HowExpert.com

PS...If you are also interested in becoming a HowExpert author, then please visit our website at HowExpert.com/writers. Thank you & again, all the best!

Table of Contents

Chapter 2: Bring Home the (extra) Bacon as a Basketball Referee!

Why would you officiate basketball?

Every official has their own reasons. These are some of mine.

When you hear about basketball officials, you may think back to the most recent March Madness tournament and all of the widely criticized "missed calls." If you're my wife you think of the old guys who showed up late to your volleyball matches: until she met me of course.

There are a few reasons why officiating basketball is one of my passions in life (my faith and family are the two most important): the competitive feeling you can only get from being involved in an organized sport, the comradery amongst fellow officials, extra money, and it's just plain hard to do.

Of course there are many other reasons to officiate basketball. I know plenty of officials who want to improve their coaching skills by experiencing basketball on the "dark side"; which is funny because us officials call coaching the "dark side."

Accelerated heart rate. Split second decisions. High stakes.

Playing a competitive sport brings about emotions and a certain spirit that many only feel when they're young; the select few who get paid to play get to feel this all the time! But wait, there is another avocation that gives you this same feeling.

Officiating basketball brings out the emotion that you long for in sports. Anyone who has played an organized sport knows that you can only experience the same amount of focus and passion when you're between the lines and the clock is running. Officiating does that for many a retired athlete, but who am I kidding? They're still athletes when they put the stripes on.

Although many want to "stay connected" to the game they played in high school or college, one of the staying powers of officiating is the comradery. Imagine working all day, riding to your game, working your game, and getting home at midnight; then do it again. If you don't have brothers and sisters to commiserate, grow, and laugh with, you won't last long. Luckily the comradery of the long hours in the car, the pre-game, post-game, and post-post-game discussions makes up for the hours away from home and the difficulty involved with officiating basketball. Luckily there are some other benefits.

Who doesn't want some extra spending money? This was one of my main motivators to get me started. While in college, I played a sport, so I didn't have the opportunity to hold down a real part-time job. One day our residence life supervisor needed referees for intramurals; hey it was minimum wage for an hour of work, so I joined up. Little did I know that it would be something I could continue after college.

Although it won't make you rich, unless you're one of the select few that can officiate 100 Division I basketball games in a season, officiating can help pay down the debt, get nice Christmas gifts, or take you on your next vacation.

Most of all officiating is just plain hard to do. I take some satisfaction in knowing that I can do something that not many others are willing to do. You spend hours and hours honing in your craft that it becomes part of you.

Can you make 15 decisions in 15 seconds? Can you run 3 miles every day during the season (same amount of decisions at the same time)? Can you ignore fan comments and focus?

Even if you can't answer yes to these questions right now, you'll learn that being an official is something that takes some time and practice. With patience and perseverance, you'll learn the skills you need to be a successful basketball referee. Read my 101 tips to unlock the secrets to officiating. When you do, you'll be glad that you're doing something you love, something that keeps you fit, something that makes extra money, and most of all, you'll be proud of doing something that not many people can do.

Chapter 1: The Official guide to getting started as a referee

"Is this your first game?"

It was a cold day in January at Washington & Lee High School in Arlington. I made sure I did what the association said I needed to do: I confirmed with my partner 48 hours in advance via email and was there 45 minutes prior to game time. I knew where to park but had no clue where the gym was.

I had the uniform, the rule and case books, the bag (it has to have wheels!), and no idea what I was doing. Once I found someone to lead me to our locker room, I sat there and wondered what it was going to be like. *My first real basketball game.*

My Referee (the crew chief, or leader) was 45 minutes late; he texted me and said to go ahead and "check the book"—I was too flustered to let him know that I had no clue what "check the book" means.

I walked out of the locker room and observed the players warming up like the manual said. I walked over to both coaches and let them know that my partner was running late and that we would wait until he showed up. Looking back I know I also forgot to have a captains meeting—its not like they listen to you anyway.

To make things even better, both coaches seemed to have forgotten that I talked to them about waiting to start—they just wanted to stay on schedule for the Varsity game I guess?

Luckily on that day, the coaches never asked me if it was my "first game," but I knew they were thinking it. I don't know what can be more unnerving: knowing that you're in over your head, or everyone else knowing it too.

Fortunately that feeling quickly vanishes at the opening toss, and you have bigger things to worry about. I really wish I had this book when I first started: on that day I would've told the coaches "no" more confidently and at least I would've known how to "check the book" by reading my rule book more thoroughly.

If you do your homework and use the following tips, you'll be on your way to becoming a great basketball referee, and you might be a little more comfortable when you have your first few games.

Getting Started

#1: Reach out to someone

There are plenty of ways to get some information about becoming an official:

1. Just walk into a gym. If you're wondering about becoming an official and it's basketball season, just go up to one of the officials and ask. You'll

never be turned away because new officials are always needed.

2. Do a Google search. Type in words like "basketball officiating [your area]" or "referee in [your area]". By doing a quick search, you'll be able to find a phone number or the email to someone who can get you to the right person to talk to.

3. Ask a coach or school administrator. The people who work the most closely with the officiating assigner are the coaches and administrators (usually athletic directors), so they will usually be able to put you in contact with the right person.

#2: Ask Questions

- How will I know when my games are?
- What time do I need to be at the game site?
- What do I need to wear?
- How much will I be paid and when will I be paid?
- How far in advance do I need to contact my partner?
- Do I have a mentor?
- Where can I get a rule and case book?

Above are just few questions that you should ask once you get started. Over the years many people have said, "the only stupid question is the one you don't ask": that is especially true for officiating.

#3: *Find a mentor*

Step 1: Tell officials you are new

In this day and age many people aren't very trusting or accepting of newcomers, but in officiating newcomers are usually very welcome. When you meet officials for the first time, tell them you're new and keep an eye out for the people who show interest in helping you or giving advice.

Step 2: Try to remember names

Some people are better at remembering names and faces than others, but try your best to remember names because you'll need to know a person's name to have a mentor/mentee relationship with them.

Step 3: Ask someone who you think you can trust and make sure they are knowledgeable

Mentors are just like everything else in the world: there are some good ones and some bad ones. When you meet officials listen in on conversation to see who knows what they're talking about and who has a good attitude about the game. Just a little hint: the person who talks the most may not be the best mentor.

You want to have a mentor that is knowledgeable about officiating. You want a mentor who isn't judgmental. You want a mentor who will take the time to work with you. You want a mentor who will answer your questions, no matter how "simple" they are.

When you find that person, just ask: "will you mentor me" or "will you help me out?"

Step 4: Ask questions

As a new official, there are going to be plenty of things that you don't know, so ask questions. A lot of questions. You'll learn a lot by just writing down questions as they come and then asking your mentor.

Step 5: Listen

If you have questions, listen to the whole answer. It goes against human nature but actually listening, and not thinking while someone else is talking, will allow you to answer your questions and form new ones.

In addition to the questions you'll ask, your mentor will probably tell you some things they think you need to know: listen. You may not think what they're saying is important right now, but it will matter eventually.

#4: Decide which level to officiate (recreation, high school)

Did you play basketball? Do you have kids playing basketball? Have you coached before? All of these questions will help you decide where to start your officiating journey.

If you just finished your playing career, in either high school or college, you probably want to start officiating high school right away; you would still referee recreation basketball for experience, but being a former player will make working high school very manageable.

If you have kids playing and just want some extra cash, you may want to start with recreation first. Many times when people approach assigners about refereeing, they think they should go straight into the biggest thing; which for them means high school, but many times you're not ready for that level of play.

If you're a coach trying to improve your rule knowledge and broaden overall basketball IQ, becoming a referee is a great option! Unfortunately its hard to balance being a referee and being a coach at the same time, especially if you're a high school coach: starting off working recreation would be your best bet.

#5: *Purchase the uniform and necessities*

Step 1: What to purchase

Find out what the uniform requirements are for the level you're working. Most state high school associations have specific shirts with patches they require you to wear to officiate sanctioned games. Different associations also have specific types of pants and pre-game warmup jackets they want you to purchase. If you're just doing recreation, ask if they allow regular striped shirts and shorts. You're definitely going to need these items:

- Predominantly black running shoes
- Black socks
- A striped shirt (some states they are grey)
- Black referee pants
- Black shorts
- A "pea-less" whistle
- A bag (it needs to have wheels!)

Step 2: Where to get it

Ask an official or your assigner if they recommend a place to purchase the gear. Many times word-of-mouth is the best way to get something so specific like the referee uniform. Ask what sites they've used and if there is a specific site to buy your state shirt.

Step 3: Get your biggest bang for your buck

Search online for the best deals! There are copious amounts of referee-gear websites out there; you just have to pick one that meets your budget.

#6: Pay association fees

"The deadline is (insert arbitrary date that is the most inconvenient for you)."

If you're becoming a member of an association or "board" of officials, you need to pay your dues: literally and figuratively (we'll get to that later). Although it may seem counter intuitive, you have to spend money to make money, so you have to pay your association dues to get on the court.

For a certified high school board, your fees may vary from $25 to $75 a year. Don't worry: these pay for themselves and the fees do have a purpose. After about 20 games of coaches and fans telling you that you're worthless, you'll appreciate those dues when they pay for the end of year banquet.

Besides the banquet, your fees go towards renting the meeting spaces, retaining legal representation for the association, scheduling software, commissioner fees, and other miscellaneous items.

What should you expect?

#7: *Manage the travel*

Step 1: Know where you're going well before you get in the car.

After you've read the schedule and confirmed your game(s) with your partner(s), you need to find out where the game is and how long it will take you to get there.

Step 2: Go prepared

There is nothing worse than getting to a gym in nowheresville and realizing you forgot your snack or worse: you don't have the gas to get home. Make sure you have water, something to eat, and at least a quarter of a tank; your body will thank you on the ride home and you won't have to hitch-hike to get home.

Step 3: Ride with your partner

You may think you can stay awake through anything, but after a 6 game day, 2 hours from home, you better think again. Many a referee have succumbed to the humdrum of the road or a stray deer, so try to ride with your partner if possible and have coffee ready.

Step 4: Pay the extra dollar (or dollars)

When you get the presorted, junk mail from your satellite radio provider or have the opportunity for the optional add-on, go ahead and pay for it. When you spend hours in your vehicle going from one game to the next, it's the little things that can make or break your mood.

#8: Expect Respect and No Respect, all at the same time

This may be the toughest tip of all: expect no respect on the court but tons of if off the court. When you tell someone at work or at the store that you're a referee, you're sure to get responses like, "there's no way I could do that" or "it takes a special personality to do that." While their statements may be true, if those same people are coaches, expect to see someone quite different.

You're entering into a competitive game, and with competition comes emotion: most of that emotion will be directed at you. No matter how hard you prepare, you're going to look "new" your first few games—

probably your first few seasons for that matter! Coaches and players will test you, but you will learn to use other's emotions to make your officiating better.

Being "First Game Ready"

#9: Get in shape

Hopefully you already incorporate exercise into your daily, or weekly, routine, but if you have a few pounds that you need to lose or don't run regularly, you need to get in your running shoes. The game of basketball is fast paced and lasts for a while— rec. games can last from 30-40 minutes of game time (60-75 minutes total) and high school games are 32 minutes of game time (90 minutes total).

There is no secret formula to being in "First Game Shape," but as long as you can sustain an elevated heart rate for 20 minutes, you're well on your way to making it look easy. Most "big time" officials have a daily workout regimen and work 5-6 games a week, but rest assured: a few days of cardio will get you ready to work on the weekends.

#10: Get in "The Books"

Step 1: Go buy the books. There are three of them.

Assuming you're starting your basketball journey in high school or below, you have three books that you need, and they're all published by the National Federation of High Schools (NFHS for short): the Official's Manual which is published every two years, the Rules Book, and the Casebook (we will get to the Official's Manual in a second). You can purchase these on Amazon or Referee.com, but many times they will be included in your dues to your association.

Step 2: Make a plan

The books around hundreds of pages, so you need a game plan to read it all. Reading your books cover-to-cover in a few sittings won't be enough to actually remember the rules and situations you need to know. If you make a goal to read for 15-30 minutes a day for three weeks, you will have read almost everything in each book.

Step 3: Read the books

The Rule book states the explicit rules of the game; the Casebook uses situations to explain and clarifies the rules. The Casebook and Rule book use Rule.Section-Article (4.4-1) as their format, and they complement each other—a specific rule will have multiple situations represented in the Casebook.

The rules of basketball are separated into 10 Rules. Make goals to read one or two sections of each rule at a time. Read the Casebook alongside the Rules book. Do not make the mistake of reading them one at a time: this will create a lot of confusion with exceptions and special, or unusual, situations that you may see in your first game.

Step 4: Ask questions

Referees that have officiated for a decade will tell you they are still learning the rules; many say that no one can truly "master" the rules and apply them, but this should be your goal. The only way to achieve this is to ask questions and learn to use rulebook language when communicating with partners, coaches, players, and other officials.

#11: Practice your mechanics (or signals)

Step 1: Read the Official's Manual

There are two main sections to the Official's Manual: Crew of 2 (2-person or 2 officials) and Crew of 3 (3-person or 3 officials). If you are working your first game in a recreation league (rec. league) or high school (HS), you will most likely work 2-person, so this is where you need to spend the most time reading.

Step 2: Practice you signals

Find a mirror. Seriously. Go to the mirror and mimic the signals which are found in the back of the rulebook or official's manual. It will feel awkward for a long time and expect to get made fun of by your roommate or family: it pays off though when you look confident on the court.

Step 3: Ask questions

Take a picture or video of you practicing your signals and show it to your mentor or another official whose opinion you respect. They will give you pointers on ways to improve and general tips.

#12: Confirm your game

Whether it is through text, email, or phone call, make sure you contact your partner a few days in advance and get a response back; there is nothing worse than working a game by yourself because your partner is at the wrong gym at the wrong time, or vice versa.

Keep your message short, sweet, and to the point. Make sure you include the date (and day of the week), the location, game time, and the time you plan to be there. You may not have met your partner, or partners, before, so it is good to include your name with a little greeting.

Here is a generic message: "Hello my name is Mike. I want to confirm our game on Monday, February 30th at No Respect High School with a start time of 7:30pm. I plan to be there at 7:00pm. Looking forward to it!"

#13: Be on time

There is nothing worse than the feeling that you get when you're running late. Make sure that you give yourself enough travel time and a little extra for traffic—a good rule of thumb is for every hour of travel time, add 10 minutes.

One of the things that you'll learn as an official is to be professional at all times: off the court and on the court. If you're late for your game and the participants are waiting on you, don't expect applause when you get there.

#14: Get ready to learn

Step 1: Start a journal

Most successful referees keep a journal in their bag. Many people learn through putting their experiences and questions on paper so they can refer to it later.

Write notes about rules, special situations, funny stories, and questions you have. Always make sure to at least write the date and who your partner was: your mind will learn to remember certain situations or "plays" when you have a reference to think back on.

Some referees journal every single game, a few games when they remember, or just when they have a specific question or learning point, but regardless: get a journal and make memories.

Step 2: Have an open mind

Officiating is one of the most rewarding avocations of all time if you approach it with the right attitude. If you keep an open mind, ask questions, and are willing to learn, you will enjoy this hobby that can make you money and keep you fit.

Step 3: Block out the noise

Honestly, being a referee isn't for everyone. It is debateable, but basketball is probably the hardest sport to officiate because of its proximity to fans and fast pace. You will hear all sorts of comments from coaches and players, which you can penalize using the rules, but the worst can definitely be from the fans.

Just remember that you're working basketball for a reason, and most importantly, they don't heckle you at the bank!

Block out the noise and focus on the task at hand.

Step 4: Have fun

Once you blow the whistle for the first time and everyone looks to you for a ruling, you won't regret all the preparation that it took to get there. Enjoy it.

Chapter 2: Bring Home the (extra) Bacon as a Basketball Referee!

In life most things revolve around money. There is no way around it. Sure we can hold to our morals and stick to our faith, but we also have to pay bills. And just because we have to pay bills and perform work to earn money, doesn't mean we need to sacrifice our morals or stick to our faith.

One of the great benefits to being a referee is extra income. There are a lot of extra benefits like exercise and doing something you enjoy, but extra income is something that is tangible; you can track how much you've made and make some serious life changes by using the extra income in a smart way.

These tips will help you manage the extra income you'll bring in as a successful basketball referee. It isn't as simple as taking the check to the bank and spending: you have to create a plan and then execute that plan. Use your officiating income how you see fit, but following these tips will start you off on the right foot.

How much are we talking?

#15: Determine your worth

Basketball is a great sport to officiate because it is played all year round. If you set your mind to it, you can work all year, and with that comes decisions: which games do I work and how do I make sure I'm compensated for my time and talent?

Step 1: Gauge the level of basketball

You must find out what level basketball you are going to work. If you are working an all-star game with college prospects from three states, you should expect to be paid more than you would a 12U girls game.

Step 2: Evaluate your worth and be reasonable

Are you an average referee that struggles to get games? You may want to lower your rate, but if you just finished working a HS state tournament, then you deserve to be paid a little more.

Step 3: Don't be afraid to say no

If you are a highly sought after official in your area and you have multiple assigners asking you to work, prioritize travel, compensation, and who you're working for. Once you set your priorities, you are probably going to say no to someone. Even if you just want a day off with your family, or you made other plans, just be honest with your assigners.

#16: Always ask how much you will be paid

As an independent contractor, you never want to walk in without knowing how much you're getting paid.

Step 1: Recognize the fact that officiating is a business

You have to internalize this simple fact: this is a business. People are paying you to give them a product, and that product is your officiating skills. Don't think you're hurting someone's feelings when you are advocating for fair compensation.

Step 2: Be blunt

Since all stakeholders (assigners, coaches, administrators, and officials) know that this is a business, they aren't going to expect you do to the work for free: so just ask how much per game.

Of course there are other motivations for officiating (competitiveness, staying in the game, working with kids, etc.), but it is a business and there is money to be made.

Step 3: Ask how you will be paid

Will you be paid via direct deposit? Then they need your banking information. Will they give you cash? Make sure you receive payment before you leave. Will they write you a check? Make sure they have your full name, it is spelled correctly, and the check is signed.

If the school or assigner says they will mail your check, make sure they have your address and ask when you should expect it in the mail.

#17: *Make a contract, either written or verbal*

*Legal disclaimer: this is advice from an official, NOT legal advice. Consult your attorney on all legal matters.

If you work for an association or conference, they negotiate the contract for you, but if you are working AAU or rec. league, you'll need to have at least a verbal contract.

Step 1: Establish what rules will be used

The rules of the game are what protects you legally. Make sure you know of any "house rules" that will be used and you get them on paper.

Step 2: Agree to a rate

Make sure that you and the other party (coordinator, coach, administrator) agree to the rate that you will be paid.

Step 3: Establish how you will be paid

Ensure how you will be paid: cash, check, or direct deposit. If you're being paid cash, it should be paid on arrival or at half time. The same applies to payment with check unless they are mailing it. If they are paying you through direct deposit, clarify when that will be paid.

Pay the Tax Man

* Disclaimer: The author is not a financial professional, nor an expert in tax law. Do your research and consult a tax professional for legal advice.

#18: Track your income

Step 1: Establish a system

Nothing is worse than trying to find something that you need. It will be especially frustrating when the IRS comes to audit you, and you don't have proper records of your income.

Whether you write down your income on a sheet of paper, use Microsoft Excel, or print bank statements, you need to have a system that keeps track of when, where, and how much you were paid.

Step 2: Update your records regularly

There is nothing worse than updating records for hours at a time. If you update your records every game you receive, or at least weekly, this will be a manageable task.

Step 3: Stick to a system

Once you have a system that works, stick with it. The more repetition that you use, the easier it will be to keep track of; don't change your system just to change it.

Step 4: Keep your records for at least three years.

IRS rules state that you should keep tax records for at least 3 years: this is how far back they can audit you.

#19: Track your expenses

Step 1: Do your research

Read up on IRS regulations for small businesses, sole proprietors, and/or independent contractors. There are many things that you need to know and keep track of in order to make money from officiating.

Step 2: Know what the qualified expenses are and what aren't

Here are a few things that are considered business expenses for officiating:

- Vehicle mileage
- Vehicle expenses (gas, maintenance, vehicle depreciation)
- Tolls
- Hotels
- Flights

- Other transportation
- Food (only 50% and if it occurs away from your "tax home")
- Association dues
- Liability Insurance
- "Equipment"
- Other expenses (seriously: talk to a CPA)

Step 3: Track your mileage

Go to your local office supply store and purchase a mileage book. Every time you travel to a game, write down the odometer mileage; when you return home, write down the odometer mileage one more time. When you complete your taxes, you can use the current IRS mileage deduction for your vehicle.

Step 4: Keep receipts

If you don't have a receipt for the expense, you cannot deduct it on your taxes. Plain and simple. Stash a small envelope in your car or in your desk at home labeled with the year and put your receipts there.

Step 5: Remember the adage "You have to spend money to make money"

There is a reason you can deduct certain expenses from your taxes: you need some items and services to run your "business" and make money. Don't be afraid to pay for something that you need; just make sure you keep that receipt.

#20: *Put money away*

Step 1: Keep records

If you are following the previous two tips, you can estimate your tax burden. Once you know your "net gain/loss," you can estimate how much tax you need to save.

Step 2: Establish a savings account

Create a savings account that you use for taxes. If you use an account that is also for your "day job," ensure that you keep track of how much goes into savings for officiating.

Step 3: Make monthly deposits

Once you know a good estimate of your tax burden and you have an account to put it in, you need to put the money away. A good ballpark number for taxes is 25% of your income. The worst thing that can happen is having to pay exactly what you saved.

Step 4: Don't touch the savings

Once you have saved money for tax purposes, just forget about it. If you withdraw from that account and don't have enough to pay your taxes, well you don't want that.

#21: Filing taxes

Step 1: Compile your records

Whether everything is on paper or digital, you need to collect everything you need: 1099s, records of payment, receipts, previous tax returns, vehicle information, etc.

Step 2: Decide if you'll use an accountant or tax preparation software

Are you savvy with numbers? Do you have some free time on your hands? Are you patient? If you can answer "yes" to those three questions, you may want to use tax preparation software. Otherwise, go to a Certified Public Accountant (CPA) to file your taxes. Your childhood friend who has done their taxes before is not a professional. Do some research and ask around for a legitimate CPA.

Step 3: Report honestly

This goes without saying, but there are plenty of people who try to gain advantages that they're not entitled to. Report what you have records and receipts for.

Step 4: File before the deadline

Know when the deadline to file with the IRS and your state is.

Step 5: Maintain your records

The IRS has rules on how long to keep your tax return and any related documents. Create a file and put it away; if digital, ensure that it is backed up on multiple devices.

How to handle extra income

#22: Separate your personal income and officiating income

Ideally you should have a checking account that has money from your "day job" to pay for your rent/mortgage, bills, and other spending. It is also good to have a personal savings for emergencies or future purchases. Continue to have these accounts, but don't use them for your officiating income.

Create the same types of accounts, except with the expectation that they are only for officiating. Do your research to find banks that have low to no maintenance fees and use that account for your officiating income and expenses. This will come in handy when tax filing season comes around, and if you're ever audited, you can keep things very neat for the auditor and create less stress for you.

#23: Decide what to spend it on

Step 1: Evaluate your priorities

There are plenty of ways to spend money and it is different for everyone. Do you can a bunch of student debt you need to pay off? Are you trying to build your emergency savings? Do you need some extra cash for holiday gifts or summer vacation?

Ask yourself these questions to get started. Once you create priorities, stick with them unless you have an emergency.

Step 2: Make sure you have enough for taxes

You read about this already, but it is worth repeating: save at least 25% for taxes. If you have extra leftover after you pay taxes, then it's time to spend it on something you want/need!

Step 3: Save & invest some of your game fees

Interest is a beautiful thing, so use it to your advantage. Instead of just putting money into a savings account that doesn't accrue much interest, put some money into an investment account that will gain more interest over time. Take a few game fees a year and place them in this account. If you save and invest continually over your officiating career, you will have a nice chunk of change at the end.

Step 4: Try not to spend it all in one place

Most financial planners will tell you to "diversify your portfolio." This basically means not to have all your eggs in one basket. Try to apply this when you go to spend your officiating income. Although it is nice to go out and buy that big ticket item, you may want to spread it out. At the end of the day, you know your financial situation, so if you want to spend it all in one place, go ahead!

How to make officiating you day job

#24: Get a real job with flexibility

Step 1: Develop a skill, and eventually a job, that will allow you some flexibility

Whether you are a good writer and want to expand that, have a financial background, or want to start your own business, try to develop something that will allow you flexibility.

You need flexibility to build your basketball schedule because eventually, you'll have to travel for games and work another job to make sure your living expenses are covered. It will take quite a few years to build your officiating schedule to a point where you can pay all your living expenses off of officiating income.

Be patient, develop a job/skill, and try to better your officiating one game at a time. You can get there.

Step 2: Make sure you're really good at your "day job"

There are going to be days where you'll need to take a few hours off here and a whole day there during basketball season. Sure you may be smart and bank all of your "comp" time or "personal" days, but taking multiple days off in a short period usually doesn't bode well with co-corkers or supervisors.

If you want to feel better about taking those days off, make sure you give your day job your absolute best every day you're there. If an employer knows you give your all and you're valuable, they won't mind as much when you take time off to follow one of your passions.

Step 3: Create a long term plan—with a financial planner

Planning to make officiating your number one source of income is risky, but if you do your due diligence, you can mitigate that risk.

Calculate your current expenses, find your net worth, take an honest look at your officiating (because you can't make it your day job unless you're really, really good), and then make some conservative estimates on how those numbers are going to change over the next _____ years: this all depends on your level of officiating, your current job, and living situation. Once you have a good grasp of your financial situation, take it to your financial planner; pay the extra money to have peace-of-mind that you're doing the right thing.

When you make this plan, try to set reasonable expectations. There is no way you can quit your day job and start officiating when you only work 30 college games a year unless you have unlimited financial resources. For most people this process may take a decade or even longer. Create your plan and make adjustments as needed.

Step 4: Constantly reevaluate your plan, and your officiating

Life happens. Sometimes things just don't work out. Priorities change.

Make sure that you constantly look back at your plan and make adjustments. If you make a plan to quit your day job in 8 years, but you've changed jobs three times and aren't making as much money, you may have to hold off on officiating full-time.

Step 5: Don't burn bridges

God forbid you go down with a career ending injury. What happens when you have to go back to a regular day job? You need to make sure you leave your day job gracefully; that way you're able to go back and make a living if the worst happens.

#25: Plan ahead

Step 1: Question fellow officials

Reach out to some fellow officials that you know well and officiate for a living. Ask them what they do to make their paychecks last the whole year and what kind of sacrifices they have to make to live comfortably.

Step 2: Evaluate the "ladder" you have to climb

Moving up in officiating is not a linear process. Many officials say that every "overnight" success took 10 years, so make sure you know what conferences you need to work in to get consistent, better paying games.

Step 3: Save, save, save

Any time you quit a job, you take a risk. Quitting your day job to do something that takes athleticism and high amounts of mental and emotional fortitude is a risk, so make sure you have plenty of money saved for the unthinkable.

#26: Make sacrifices

Step 1: Learn what you'll have to sacrifice

Time with family. A long held passion. A steady and reliable source of income. There are many things you'll have to sacrifice when you make officiating your day job. Make sure you sit down and do your research to make an informed decision.

Step 2: Communicate with your family

Make sure your family knows what to expect. They may not be able to go on that expensive vacation or get that luxury car the first few years while you build your schedule. Be honest and explicit with your family and they will support you.

Step 3: Be honest with yourself

Do you think you can make it? Do your fellow officials think you can make it your day job? If you are honest with yourself, you'll be able to make an informed decision and live out your passion in the best way you can.

Chapter 3: Working Better Basketball Games and seeing your schedule grow

More more more. In our society, it is assumed that **more** is a right. But in officiating, nothing comes as a right; you have to work hard to get the next biggest game and see your schedule grow.

Many of the tips in this book are how to handle things off the court. This chapter focuses on what you have to do for a better basketball schedule. Sure many of the tips below are things you have to do to prepare, like read your rules and watch film, but these actionable tips are what will set you apart from other referees on the court.

At the end of the day, you should want to be the person that people want to be around. If you're knowledgeable, skillful in how you officiate, and have the right attitude, you will find yourself working the next state final or tournament.

Mastering the rule book

#27: Read and reread the books

Step 1: Read the rulebook and casebook cover to cover at least twice a year.

This is a serious step. No one can know every rule after reading the rulebook and casebook once... well unless you have photographic memory. For most officials, the rules are something that take time to learn, and if you stay in the rulebook consistently, you'll become as close to a master of the rules as you can get.

Step 2: Pack your rulebook in your bag

If you talk about rules in your pregame, take out your rulebook. Say you come in the locker room at half time and had an atypical situation, take out your rulebook. If you disagree with a ruling (not a judgement call), take out your rulebook.

Step 3: Talk to fellow officials about the rules

When you "talk shop" in officiating, you are creating more connections in your brain and are learning more. When an official is describing a situation to you, ask them what rules apply. Or maybe you might give them a suggestion on how they could have ruled based on the rulebook.

Step 4: If you're the "R" or the "Crew Chief," make the rules part of your pregame

The "R" or "Crew Chief" is the leader of the crew of officials for that game. It is typically their job to conduct a pregame discussion and all the various responsibilities prior to tip-off. If you make rule review part of your pregame, you're not only advancing your knowledge; you're elevating the knowledge of the other officials on your crew.

#28: Use rulebook language

Step 1: Read the rules

It may sound redundant, but to use rule book language, you have to read and reread the rules. With that said, you don't have to memorize the rules, but you should be able to use terms from the rulebook when you speak. This takes time and practice.

Step 2: Practice using the lingo in your pregame discussion

Every game you should have a "pregame discussion." Sometimes this is just 5-10 minutes, but a thorough pregame may take 45 minutes. Regardless, have a pregame and use the language of the rulebook.

Step 3: Use rulebook language when you talk to players and coaches

There are a lot of different terms that coaches, players, fans, and commentators like to use that are completely incorrect: "over-the-back" and "she has to be set to take a charge" are just a couple examples. If you use rulebook language as a way to communicate with players and coaches, it informs them, but it also makes you sound more credible. All officials can use a boost in credibility!

#29: Find your "inner circle"

Step 1: Find some fellow officials who want to learn

Officiating can be a very lonely endeavor when you work with different partners every night and are traveling constantly: find a few fellow officials that want to continuously learn and stay in touch with them.

Step 2: Ask questions

Whether you call your "inner circle," text, or email them, ask questions about the rules. Most officials like to use casebook format to ask questions to be clear, but just describe a situation and ask for a ruling. You could also describe your situation and state how you ruled and ask for feedback.

Step 3: Communicate often

Everyone knows to nuture any kind of relationship, you need to communicate. Preseason, basketball season, and camp season can stretch for a long time, so make sure to stay in touch with your fellow officials. Plus who wants to talk shop all the time? A "how's it going?" goes a long way in a long season.

Step 4: Cite rules when you have a question

If you ask someone to make a ruling and they tell you without the rule citation, you've only made one connection. If someone tells you the ruling with a citation and you look up the rule, you've made two connections. Next thing you know you'll have thousands of connections.

Step 5: Don't be afraid to sound stupid

Basketball is a hard sport to officiate. With athletes that never get older and hundreds of pages of rules and mechanics to master, sometimes you're just not going to have the answer. If you think it's a stupid question, you'll think it's even more stupid when you don't ask and you get the rule wrong in your next game.

#30: *Join an online community*

Step 1: Ask other officials if they are a part of an online community

The best way to find a quality community of officials is word of mouth. As you work with people, you'll work with some great officials that have a lot to offer. Ask them if they are part of an online community of officials.

Step 2: Do some research

Go online and just Google "basketball officiating." You're likely to get a lot of hits, but just go through and find one that fits you. Most social media sites have groups or prominent officials that post questions and video clips of plays to learn from. Take advantage of it!

Step 3: Make an investment

Many online communities are free, but you can really learn more by joining a community that posts weekly video clips with voice overs, interview top officials, and networks with top officials across the country. Decide what a reasonable amount of money would be for you to spend per month (most times you can work one recreation game and have it paid for) and then pick a community that you feel comfortable with.

#31: *Listen to podcasts and watch videos*

Step 1: Do some research

Type in keywords for the types of plays or rules you want to learn. Many times there will be videos of basketball plays where a violation or foul wasn't called and you could learn from it.

Step 2: Set aside some time

Carve out some time each week to watch basketball plays and listen to podcasts on rules. Do these things with the rulebook, casebook, and mechanics manual and you'll be on your way to creating thousands of connections to use in your next game.

Step 3: Take notes

When you hear a quote that makes a lot of sense to you or is something you've never heard, write it down. Then go share it with a fellow official to spread the knowledge.

Mastering the "Mechanics"

#32: Pick three areas to improve every year

Step 1: Identify your weaknesses

Whether you find out your weaknesses through deep self-awareness, critiques from other officials, or film, make sure you know what the weaknesses are. Is it the way you stand on the court? Could you communicate with your partners better? Do you have strong and crisp signals? Ask yourself and others these questions to find out what your weaknesses are.

Step 2: Choose the top three things that you need to improve on

Most people whose job it is to teach something (teachers, bosses, CEOs) know that to really improve, you have to focus on a few weaknesses at a time to see results. If you have 20 things you need to improve on, you won't be able to focus and improve on any of them. Pick three things that you struggle with the most.

Step 3: Write the three things down

Somewhere, you should write the things down. Whether you use a computer or paper, just write them down so you don't forget them.

Step 4: Revisit your points of emphasis

What is the point of writing it down if you don't look at it again? Take some time daily or weekly to revisit your points of emphasis. Evaluate yourself to see if you're improving or if you need to do something differently.

Step 5: Share your points of emphasis with your partners

In pregame, tell your partner what you're working on. "I'm working on communicating where the spot throwin is every time I blow my whistle." Then ask your partner how you did with that. The worst thing they can say is "I didn't notice anything." The best thing that could happen is you get an outside perspective and learn something.

#33: Read the manual

Step 1: Read the manual

Pretty simple stuff. Just read the manual.

Step 2: Make notes

If you're keeping a journal, this would be a great place to take notes on positioning, partnering, and primary coverage areas.

Step 3: Ask questions

In your pregame, pick a few mechanics that you want to work on. For example, ask your partner, "if it's a C-side drive, who has a primary whistle on the foul at the basket?" This can create great discussion, even if you already know the answer. Ask questions especially if you're not sure of the correct mechanic to use.

#35: *Practice perfectly*

Step 1: Find a mirror

You would be surprised how many mirrors there are in the world! Look around your house and you'll have at least five. All bathrooms have them... Plus most gyms and recreation centers have dance rooms that are great places for solitary practice.

Step 2: Signal in front of the mirror

Go to the signals section of the official's manual. Then practice the signals in front of the mirror. It may seem awkward, but the more muscle memory you create, the more credible you'll be on the court.

Step 3: Practice it perfectly

When you practice, make sure every repetition is exactly correct. A lot of bad habits can be avoided by making sure you use correct signals that are crisp.

#35: *Ask for feedback or critiques*

Step 1: Find out who is on the game after yours

Whether you have the JV game or you have someone officiating after you on the same court in rec leagues, find out who is on the game. Call or email your assigner and tell them you want feedback and ask who is coming behind you; they'll usually get back to you with a name, and hopefully, their number.

Step 2: Ask the official to watch you

Saying something as simple as, "hey would you mind watching me for a few minutes and tell me some things I can work on?" is a great conversation starter. There's this funny thing about human nature; people like to share their opinions, or "wisdom." Take advantage of that and have a fresh set of eyes watch you.

Step 3: Be specific when you ask for feedback

The more specific you can be when you ask a fellow official to watch you, the better. If you ask someone to watch for something, they will focus on it immediately. For example, if you're trying to work on getting your hand up to "stop the clock," tell that official, and they will immediately notice if you do not signal correctly.

Step 4: Follow up

After your game, ask the official who watched you specific questions. Write down their feedback. If there is a quick turnaround for game times, make sure to give them a call or text to ask how you did and what they suggest you need to do to improve.

#36: Go to camp

Step 1: Ask other officials and do some research

During spring and summer, there are many "travel basketball" tournaments, and these tournaments need officials. Ask officials if they know of a good "teaching camp" nearby. You could also search online for "basketball officiating camps."

Step 2: Save some money

Camps can cost anywhere from $50 to $500, so decide what your budget is and stick to that. Also remember that there might be other costs associated with the camp like travel, lodging, and food. If you take a couple game fees and save them, you're well on your way to paying for your first camp!

Step 3: Go to camp and be a sponge

Go prepared by reading all the materials the organizer sends you and read the official's manual. Then take copious notes, ask questions, and listen. At this camp you'll likely get some classroom instruction, but the most valuable is on-court instruction. Listen to the evaluators and learn from the feedback they give you, and your fellow campers.

#37: Mentor a new official

Step 1: Gain some experience

Officiating is a business, and with any business, the more experience you have, the better off you are. Once you gain some name recognition and other officials know who you are, be open to mentoring brand new officials.

Step 2: Offer your opinion... when asked

No one likes a know-it-all, so make sure that you wait until you're asked before you start sharing your "wisdom" with new officials. If you offer up too much advice, then you risk the chance of being written off as a know-it-all, and then you won't be much help to new officials.

Step 3: Stay in touch

When you have a brand new official who is asking questions and is wanting to learn, give them your contact info to continue the conversation. Tell them you're happy to answer any questions they have, and they'll usually oblige.

"I've got a great partner tonight"

#38: Be a good partner

In officiating, you want to be the person who everyone wants to work with. When you create a persona that people respect and admire, your games will go more smoothly.

In general, being a good partner is just about being a good person. If you're considerate and humble, with some knowledge thrown in there, you will be someone who other officials look forward to working with.

#39: Over communicate

A great official once told me that if you think you're communicating too much, it is probably enough. If you think you're communicating enough, you're probably not. This is a good maxim to live by.

Whether it is identifying the shooter, signaling to your partner when you'll reach the bonus with the next foul, signaling how many free throws should be given, or designating the spot of the throw-in, communicate with volume and confidence. You're much more likely to have a smooth game if you "over communicate."

#40: Leave your baggage, but not your bag, at home

Life happens. You had a bad day at work; you couldn't find your best pair of running shoes in the closet; you didn't have enough time to pack a snack; you're having financial trouble at home.

All of these things happen, and they might even happen on the same day. Even so, when you come into the locker room, focus on the task at hand. If you're really having trouble, tell your partner that you've got a lot going on, but that you're ready to be a good partner that night.

#41: Contribute to pregame discussion

Step 1: Have a pregame

Whether you're the "U1," "U2," or the "R," you should initiate a pregame discussion. Typically the "R" leads the discussion, but sometimes that won't happen and you'll need to step up and start talking.

Step 2: Come prepared

Some crew chiefs will tell their U1 and U2 to prepare a review of certain rules. Sometimes you can share video clips. Whatever you do, come prepared with something to talk about.

Step 3: Ask questions

When you're in the locker room, it is a great place to get to know your partners. Ask them a general personal question or two if you don't know them. Then get down to business and ask what they'd do in a certain situation on the court.

Step 4: Be honest

If you had a really bad situation the other night and you "kicked" a rule, tell them; there is always something to learn from in mistakes. If you're struggling with a certain judgment call, tell your partners. If you have points of emphasis, or areas of weakness, that you are trying to improve upon, tell you partners and be honest.

#42: *Have high expectations*

When you develop high expectations, you elevate the crew. If you approach partnering in a way that has high expectations with grace, you'll be a sought after partner. Approach every night with high expectations of your crew, and be honest with them after the game. Honestly you're not going to meet your expectations every night and that's ok. Have the grace to learn from it and move on to the next game.

#43: *Give respectful criticism*

Step 1: Be self-critical

Point out the mistakes you made in the game. No referee has ever officiated a "perfect game." If you give an honest self-assessment, then your partners are going to be more willing to hear what you have to say.

Step 2: Know your audience

Are you talking to a "seasoned" veteran? (you'll meet many officials who have a lot of "experience," but it is the wrong kind of experience) Or are you talking to a brand new official? Does this official have a reputation?

The answers to those questions are going to determine how, or if, you are going to give constructive criticism.

Step 3: Pick a few things

If you are critiquing a brand new official, pick three things that you'd like to communicate to them.

If you are critiquing a "veteran" or someone who isn't new, pick one thing.

If the official has a great attitude and is asking for more feedback, then give as much feedback as they are comfortable with.

Step 4: Start with a question

"Can you walk me through that play?" is a great way to start a conversation. Maybe the official had a different angle on the play. Maybe they have misinterpreted a rule or don't even know the rule.

Hearing their thoughts on the play will guide you in your response, but whatever you do, don't ask: "What did you see?" This question automatically puts officials on the defensive and effectively ends any learning opportunity.

Step 5: Respond with humility

No one likes a know it all, but everyone like being given respect.

When you give a critique, try to remember that you're essentially making a judgement on that person's officiating. Read their body language and gauge how they respond to see how you continue.

If your critique causes your fellow official to ask questions, great! Keep the discussion going and use the rulebook, casebook, and official's manual to help them (and yourself) improve.

If the official's non-verbal ques, or defensive words, suggest they don't agree or they just say "okay," it is time to move on and discontinue the critique or feedback discussion.

The Eye in the Sky Doesn't Lie

#44: Get the film

Getting film on your games can be a tall order. If you're officiating rec leagues or "travel basketball," this can get tricky. Those types of games are rarely filmed by teams, but you can always bring your camera and set it up. Even better if you can convince a friend to spend an hour or two filming your game.

If you're officiating high school, the teams are almost always filming. If you're comfortable, send the coach a two sentence email asking for the film, and make sure not to ask for feedback in any way: this is pandering and does not bode well for your impartiality as a game official.

If you're officiating in college, you'll most likely have access to a database with your games. Make sure to download your games soon after and get to it when you can.

#45: *Watch the film*

Step 1: Set aside some time to watch the film

The hardest part of watching film to learn and get better is finding the time to do it. Between working, having a family, and working basketball games, it's hard to fit it all in. Set aside a couple hours each week (or even more!) to review your game film.

Step 2: Use the pause button

Just watching film straight through without stopping is a waste of time. The pause button is your friend. When you get to a foul or violation in the film, pause it to check the crew's positioning. Don't spend a lot of time validating calls though; the fact that you're correct or incorrect is pretty obvious, so the real learning point is your positioning, game management, rule application, court presence, and signaling.

Step 3: Focus on mechanics

Did you make a switch correctly? Are you "position adjusting" or "moving to improve" your angles on the court to see between players? Are you officiating in your primary coverage area and not "ball watching?"

These are all good questions to ask yourself, but it is not an exhaustive list. Use your points of emphasis, or areas of weakness, as the basis of watching film.

Step 4: Fast forward

It is definitely important to watch how you "dead ball officiate," but once there isn't any action going on in the game and there is a slight pause in the action (like in between free throws or a long substitution), press the fast forward button. Watching an hour and thirty minutes of game film can turn into three hours if you don't use the fast forward button on unimportant times.

Step 5: Fast forward again

Once you've watched a certain part of the film where you had some questionable judgement calls, use fast forward to see things happen at a fast pace. This can help train your eyes to differentiate between incidental (legal) contact and illegal contact.

#46: Clip plays

Step 1: Learn how to do it

Ask someone or do a quick online search to find out how to "clip," or make a short clip from a long video, you'll want to clip certain plays that are good learning points.

Step 2: Develop a system

Create a folder on your computer for clips. Organize a system where you can you're your clips in some type of logical order. Whether you do it by mechanics, the position you call from, or the type of violation or foul it is, find a system to save them, so the clips are easier to locate later.

#47: Be your own worst critic

If you want to improve and get better games, you have look at yourself with a critical eye on film. Getting better means making positive changes, and change can only come if you know what you did wrong.

Are you slouching when you settle in the front court? Does your run look unathletic? Do your signals look lazy? These are all questions you'll have to ask yourself, so the key is to be honest with yourself.

Yeah sure it is neat to see yourself on camera, and definitely give yourself a pat on the back when you do something right! But most of your time needs to be spent by critically looking at your performance and appearance on the court.

#48: Share the film

Step 1: Stay organized

If you followed the previous tips on clipping the film, you should be able to find a clip quickly. This will save a lot of time and energy.

Step 2: Know what medium to share with

There are many ways to share clips whether it is on a type of online dropbox, through email, or text. Pick one of the mediums that works best for you.

Step 3: Reach out to your inner circle

If you followed the tip on finding an "inner circle," it's time to reach out to them using film. Share film and ask questions. What could I have done better? How could I have handled the situation differently? What would you have ruled? Using these questions with your film will help you and your inner circle become better officials.

Chapter 4: Paying your dues (figuratively)

Official A: "How's your season going?"

Official B: "It's going great, I can't complain at all. How about you?"

Official A: "Well you know how it is. I've got 7 in a row this week. First I'm going to PH, then I've got LB, then he's sending me all the way to Highlands, then I go to Averett which is $200, can you believe that? Then I have Flemming, and Staunton on Saturday, then I'm working some AAU on Sunday."

Official B: (Sigh…) *It's going to be a long night…*

There is nothing more frustrating than working with Official A. They usually mean well, but in my experience, after a season of conversations like that, they don't have "7 in a row" anymore.

Official A, good for you, but talking about your schedule won't win you many friends, and you sure won't be working those games for very long if you brag to every partner you work with.

Be honest, but also be humble. This is great advice that was impressed upon me early in my journey. This concept applies to just about every facet of life. Talking about your schedule too much is only one of the unwritten rules that you'll need to internalize in your officiating journey. These tips will help you navigate the uncertain waters of the politics behind officiating and ensure that you are respected other officialsyou're your assigners.

Know where your bread is buttered

#49: Develop great relationships

Step 1: Be approachable

Smile. Laugh. Ask questions.

If you're always serious and don't ask questions, then people won't want to be around you. Carry yourself, on and off the court, in a way that makes people want to be around you. The on-court part of basketball officiating is only half the journey, so make sure when you're off the court, you're approachable.

Step 2: Learn who people are

Learning names and faces can be tough, especially when you can potentially work with someone different every night.

When you work a game with someone, write down their name and something unique about them (occupation, the car they drive, or where they're from). This will help you remember them the next time you work with them.

Step 3: Get phone numbers

If you work with someone, you'll automatically get their phone number since you have to confirm your game with them. But what about the officials that you see at meetings or the ones that have a game before or after yours?

When you meet a fellow official that you're not working with, get their contact information. This increases the chances of you actually remembering their name, and getting their contact info gives you another person to add to your "inner circle."

Step 4: Don't be afraid to ask people their names

You'll end up working with a lot of different people. It is okay if you forget someone's name. Just ask them to remind you what their name is.

#50: Stay connected

Step 1: Make friends

Officiating can be a lonely business if you don't make some friends. Long drives and time away from home can be assuaged by having a group of officials you can talk to and stay connected with.

Step 2: Know who you need to stay in touch with

There are certain people who you need to know and stay in touch with, so find out who those people are. They might be your board members of your local association. They might be assignors for a nearby conference. Or they might be a really good official who can speak to your abilities.

Regardless you have to accept that there are some "politics" in officiating. Don't pander or "brown nose," but don't avoid the fact that there are certain people you need to know.

#51: Be honest with your assigners and fellow officials

"Honesty is the best policy" definitely applies to officiating, but this only applies when you're talking about your actions, or opinions, towards others (sometimes you may want to withhold a critique of an official). For example, if you have a couple different assigners you work games for in the summer and one schedules you first, don't be afraid to tell the others that you're already working for that assigner.

There is nothing worse than creating some lie that you're off somewhere else when you're actually working for another assigner; they talk, and they will find out. If you're honest, you'll earn their respect.

If a fellow official asks you a question, be honest and give them your opinion. Simple.

#52: Keep your goals in mind

Where you want to end up as a basketball official dictates a lot of your actions. Do you want to stay near home and just make some extra money? Do you want to work the Final Four one day? Do you want to work Game 7 of the NBA finals?

Whenever you're making a decision about how you interact with supervisors, assigners, and fellow officials, you need to remember that you have goals.

#53: Respect your assigners/supervisors

Step 1: Take some time to get to know your assigner

Whether you just moved into an area, you're trying out at a camp, or they just come by one of your games, you need to get to know your assigner. It's human nature to be inquisitive, so just be yourself and ask questions. What do you do for a living? Do you still officiate? How did you get into officiating? Do you have kids?

All are great questions to ask, but just talk to them. They may make your schedule, but don't be afraid of them. If they know you care then they won't just see you as a number or a slot to fill.

Step 2: Learn their pet peeves

Assigners do a lot of work behind the scenes in scheduling, communicating with coaches and administers, and making sure officials get paid. You do not want to make their job harder, so make sure you cross your Ts and dot your Is.

Some assigners are sticklers for professionalism and want to be addressed a certain way. Some want to be called after every game if you're the R (crew chief). Ask other veteran officials what the assigner's pet peeves are and you'll have a good idea of what not to do.

Step 3: Contact them every now and then

You are one of hundreds of officials that your assigner works with, so don't call or text them every day of the week. If you haven't talked to them in a few weeks and your blocks changed, give them a call to let them know you're open if they have an emergency and need someone to cover a game.

Step 4: When they ask for something, do it

Obviously you have a life, so you're not always going to be able to say yes to everything. When your assigner calls you last minute to work a game, try to be flexible and work the game: don't say you're not available because you have tickets to the local minor league hockey game or had a late night the night before.

The little things do matter

#54: For God's sake, keep your schedule to yourself

Regardless of where you are in life, you should listen twice as much as you talk. This doubly applies to officiating when you talk to other officials about schedules. If you're giving a detailed outlook of your schedule, you're mostly just filling in conversation and the other official doesn't care.

At best they may feign interest in hearing all the games you have, but at worst, much much worse, you get a reputation for being ego-driven and hard to work with.

#55: Take care of your "blocks"

Step 1: Know your assigner's expectations

No matter how your assigner takes care of scheduling (online or paper/pencil), you need to find out what they expect you to do.

Do they want you to individually block the days and times you're working your day job, or do they just want you to block out night times if you're not available? If you block a night because you're working for Assigner A, does Assigner B want to know who/where you're working?

Knowing what they expect of you will ensure that you stay in good graces and get more opportunities on the court.

Step 2: Have a plan for your blocks

Everyone is different, so you need to know your situation and how many nights a week you can work. If you have a consistent work commitment every Tuesday, make sure you block every Tuesday. If you work four 12 hour shifts in a row and know that you need a complete day to rest, make sure you block that day.

Besides work commitments, variable family schedules, and rest days, there are certain days that never change and there's no excuse for not blocking them: your birthday, other birthdays, anniversaries, the Superbowl, Memorial Day, Valentine's Day.

Step 3: Keep your blocks updated

Nothing bothers an assigner more than not keeping your blocks updated: this is a great way to reduce your schedule in the future.

For example, it's Monday and you weren't assigned a game for Friday. You decide to have a date night with your significant other because you haven't spent a lot of time with each other lately. After you've confirmed your plans, your assigner gives you a game for Friday.

Now you have to "turn it (the game) back." That means calling the assigner and telling them that you're not available. Their expectation is that you keep your blocks updated, so reassigning the game is just one more thing out of the thousand that they have to do. Moral of the story: don't make their life harder.

#56: Develop a priority list

Step 1: Make a list of all your conferences

If you work in an urban area with multiple officials' boards, you might work for a few different assigners. If you work high school and college, you definitely have multiple assigners and supervisors.

Sit down and make a list of them. Simple

Step 2: Decide what is important to you

Do you want to gain experience? Do you want to "move up"? Do you want to stay close to home? Do you want to make the most money you can?

All of these questions can help guide you in deciding what is important to you. Hopefully at some point in your career you'll have two or three assigners who want you on the same night; what is important to you will help you decide which league to work that night.

Step 3: Give your assigners/supervisors your list

Only do this if they ask for a priority list. If you're lucky, your assigners will have a good relationship and will work together so you're not in the middle. If they don't ask for your list, that's fine; just use it to make decisions on your blocks and schedule.

Step 4: Stick to the list

Once you create your list and give it to an assigner, you should probably stick to that list unless you have a huge life event like a death in the family, you lost a job, or have children. Just stick it out until next season and change your list to match your changing priorities.

#57: Follow the written and unwritten rules

Step 1: Read the policies/by-laws

If you work in an officials association, it will have by-laws. If you work for an assigner that works for a specific organization or conference, then they should have specific policies pertaining to officiating. If you're just doing your local church a favor, know who to contact in case of emergency or how you'll be paid.

Step 2: Know the "unwritten" rules

- Treat each partner like they are an expert.
- Show respect to the people who are working the scoreboard and official scorebook.
- Don't talk to fans when you're on the court.
- Don't touch players.
- Don't talk behind other officials' backs to get an extra game.

- Don't be the official to give their first and second technical to a player or coach, if you can help it.

These are only a few examples, but if you fail to follow the "Dos" and "Don'ts," you're sure to lose games and respect within the officiating community.

Step 3: Don't "turn back" games unless absolutely necessary

Life happens. Assigners understand that people get sick, work commitments come up, and the unexpected happens, so it's okay to "turn back" a game. Just don't make it a habit for things that could be planned around: running errands, watching other sporting events, or soft plans with friends. If you need to do some of those things, just go ahead and block the day.

#58: Give back to the game

Step 1: Work some games that don't pay

There are a lot of great causes for charity out there, and sports are a great way to bring people together for a worthy cause to raise money. With events like this you won't get paid, or you'll have the option to donate your game fee, which you should do.

Step 2: Mentor an official

Once you have a few years of experience, it is time to reach down and pull another official up. If you're working a certain level of basketball, then there are other officials that want to be there too. You remember how it was being a first year official, so help them out and share your experiences with them so they can learn.

Step 3: Communicate positively with the community

As a basketball official, you're an ambassador to the game. You represent impartiality and fair play.

Make sure your verbal and non-verbal actions communicate respect for the game and its participants: there have been many officials who saw their careers come to an abrupt end because they didn't show respect to someone in the community on or off the court.

Chapter 5: Settle down big timer! You're not refereeing on TV yet!

Becoming a high level referee can be an extremely tough road, but it is worth it for those that want to be at the top of the profession, especially if you want to make officiating your "day job."

It is impossible to tell you everything you need to know to become a high-level college or professional basketball referee, but here I try to lay out the basics. Just like everyone isn't made to go to college, because we need people to work trades too, officiating at a high level isn't something that is for everyone.

How do you decide between men's college, women's college, or professional basketball?

#59: *Do your research*

Step 1: Ask other officials

When you meet an official, ask them questions. There is no manual on "moving up" in officiating, so you have to rely a lot on the experiences of others to navigate where you want to see your career go.

Step 2: Go to the internet

Assemble some keywords and search them. College Basketball Official. NBA/WNBA Referees. These are good ones to start with. From there you'll be able to find other keywords that can help you answer questions about how much money they make and what their schedules are like.

Step 3: Be patient

You won't learn everything about "climbing the ladder" in one year, or even two. It takes some time to learn who you need to know and which camps to go to. Plus if you rush your decision, you could end up working a level of basketball that you don't enjoy.

Step 4: Find leagues or conferences that are "gateways"

If your end goal is to work in Conference A, you won't start working Conference A overnight, or even in a few years.

You'll need to go to the camp that will get you hired in Conference C. Once you do well in Conference C, you'll be able to get into Conference B. After you've worked the conference tournament in Conference C and B, you might get the chance to work in Conference A.

It can be a process that takes a number of years, but that is what it takes: time, patience, and hard work with a purpose.

#60: Find out which leagues are near you

Once you have done your research about what games you need to work to move up, search the schools that are within a reasonable driving distance: not more than 5 hours. If you can get to quite a few of the schools, then it might make sense to "try out" for that conference.

#61: Create your goals based on the level you want to officiate

Step 1: Know what you want to accomplish

Do you want to officiate the highest level? Do you want to work Game 7 of the Finals? Or do you want to work the Final Four?

Asking yourself these questions will help you create goals to move forward and enjoy your officiating journey.

Step 2: Know what you have to do to "climb the ladder" in college or professional basketball

Once you have your goals, you need to know what it takes to accomplish that goal. If your goal is to work the Men's Final Four, there is a host of people who you need to get to know and work games for. There may be some conferences that will expose you to higher level play, so its better to work in those conferences rather than others.

Step 3: Combine Step 1 and 2

Once you have your goals and know what it takes, you can create your plan for moving forward. No matter what you choose, your journey may be a long one, but using these steps will ensure that you enjoy your time as a referee.

#62: Be a student of the game

Watch games on TV. Go to games that are near you on a night off. Ask your mentor if you can listen in on their pre/post game discussions.

All of these will help you be a student of the game: the game of officiating. The more you learn, the higher you'll go.

#63: Talk to your mentor about what's best for you

By the time you're making the decision between men's college, women's college, or professional, you'll have a mentor who will know you and your situation. They'll also be able to give you an honest assessment of your talent. Ask them what they think.

Let's go camping!

#64: Find out which camps to go to

Camps are how college and professional assigners/supervisors hire officials to work in their league/conference. Whether you do an internet search or ask other officials, you need to find out which camps will help you "move up."

If you're going to your first camp, try to stay within a budget and stay close to home. If you're ready to try and work Division I basketball, you need to go to the camps where you know the assigner, they know you already, and the conference has schools that are close to home.

#65: Save money for camps

Step 1: Create a plan

Once you have you goals and know which camps you want to attend, find out how much they cost and when it is. You don't want to do a bunch of work to go to a camp and come to find out you can't afford it or have a commitment that keeps you from going.

Step 2: Make money

Always try to use money you made officiating for camps; if you pay with money from your day job, you risk losing more money than you should. Have the discipline to wait for the eventual payoff. If you put an investment into camps, your games when you get hired will pay for the camp, and next year's too!

Step 3: Put away the money

If you know how much you can spend on camp, set aside that amount of money. Whether you take a percentage of each game fee or you take the first four games of the season, find a way to save enough for camp.

Step 4: Forget about it

Don't look at the savings account. Don't let them money burn a hole in your pocket.

#66: Have the right attitude

Camps are opportunities to learn. Period.

You learn rules, mechanics, and the dos and don'ts of officiating. If you go in with an attitude that is ready to learn, you will make the most out of your camp experience.

#67: Accept criticism with grace

Step 1: Become self-aware

Self-awareness is a skill that is learned over time with experience and failure. Knowing your emotions goes a long way towards keeping you positive in a situation where you're receiving criticism from someone you may not know.

Step 2: Know some of your biggest weaknesses

Go to camp with an idea of what you need to improve on as an official. If you're able to tell the evaluator, or clinician, that is watching your game some of the skills you're working on, it will give them something to focus on and give you specific feedback.

Step 3: Control your non-verbal

Your face and body language can tell someone your intentions and thoughts a lot more than your words. If you accept feedback by looking the observer in the eye and nodding with your head held high, you give the impression that you're there to learn and accept their feedback.

Step 4: Show appreciation

Always say thank you; even if you don't like what they said. Sometimes observers at the same camp will tell you two contradictory things, so it can be frustrating. Don't let that frustration show in how you interact with the clinician or your partners.

At the end of the day, the supervisor, who is running the camp and is who you have to impress, selected officials they trust to be observers for their camp. The one thing the supervisor wants to hear is if their trusted officials would work a game with you. If you accept negative feedback with grace, they'll tell the supervisor to hire you.

#68: When you do get hired, treat it as an opportunity and blessing, not a right

There are no sure things in the world. Basketball officiating is no exception. Unless it is written into law, you don't have a "right" to do anything, so you need to have that attitude going into camp.

If you treat getting hired as an opportunity, you will learn and you will be seen as someone to emulate by newer officials.

Switching between levels is hard

#69: Decide which level is most important for you

Are you wanting to move up to the next level? Do you want to work the high school state tournament? Is your dream to work the NBA Finals?

If you're lucky enough to work in multiple levels of basketball, you'll have some decisions to make on how you study your rules and how you use the prescribed signals of the levels you officiate. Depending on what is most important to you, you may have to focus on different things when you officiate.

#70: Become an expert in mechanics for each level

Read your official's manuals: every level is going to have a different one. You can't "cram" for games, or right before the season starts, by reading them in one sitting. This takes constant study that is goal focused. Try to go through the manuals side-by-side with a highlighter: as you get to a difference, go through each book and highlight it.

Using the highlighter method and by following the other tips pertaining to your books, you'll be in a good position to be knowledgeable about the mechanics.

#71: Develop a pre-game routine for each level you officiate

Step 1: Try things out

There is no set routine that ensures success. Some officials like to get to games early and meditate. Some like to spend more time grooming. Some officials like to listen to music before their pre-game discussion.

Try out different activities in differing orders to find what works for you.

Step 2: Write it down

If you have a routine, write down. When you have a routine that makes you feel prepared and comfortable on the court, you need to make sure that you try to stick to it. Sometimes you may take a few months off and forget the routine, so write it down for when you start the next season.

Step 3: Don't be afraid to change the routine

People change. Maybe one year you needed 5 minutes to warm-up; now that you're older, and have worked 1,000 games, you need 30 minutes with 10 different things to help you warm-up (heating pads, foam rollers, massagers, etc.).

If you feel like your routine doesn't help you, don't be afraid to change it.

Step 4: Be flexible

You show up an hour before tip-off. You go through your normal routine with getting dressed, having a pre-game discussion, and getting warmed up. The tip-off is on time. The game ends in a reasonable amount of time, and you drive home. This is the dream.

Buses breakdown. Partners are late. The roof in the gym leaks. There is an extended delay for an injury. Weather makes you late.

There are a whole host of problems that can throw off your routine, so you need to be prepared to just do your best and respond positively.

#72: Be humble about your schedule

If you go around talking about your schedule to people when they don't ask, you will gain a reputation. So unless someone asks you specifically about the games you're working, and the level (high school, college, etc.), keep your schedule to yourself. Don't be the official that feels like they need to mention that they "work college basketball" all the time; let your skills on the court speak for you.

Chapter 6: No one ever said officiating was easy

Wake up at 5am to walk the dog. While getting ready for work I hear, "Steven you need to stay later with the dog because I won't be home right after work." Great. That means I won't be able to make copies for my lessons for today.

So I go to work and fly by the seat of my pants; my students were crazy, but such is life as a teacher. Now it's time for a three hour drive to tonight's game.

The game was a blow-out, but I had a few good learning moments. Well it's 9:30pm, so a three hour drive, but I have to stop for food and gas. Probably home around 1am. Wake up at 5am to... And repeat.

This routine can wear you down, but the following tips will help you stay rested, give time to your family, perform well at your day job, and be a great basketball official, all at the same time.

Officiating a sport requires a tremendous amount of balance. I, like most officials, are not fortunate enough to just officiate (maybe when I retire!), and that comes with greater responsibility and stress. Finding ways to handle that responsibility can lead to many tough moments, but all you have to do is learn from them.

Family

#73: Know the difference between a hobby, avocation, and vocation

Hobby: an activity you do that brings you happiness and passes the time. Usually you have to give up your own money for a hobby.

Avocation: an activity you do that brings you happiness that you get paid to do. Avocations are something that don't always "pay off," but you make some money while doing something you enjoy.

Vocation: a vocation is your job or career that pays the bills and ensures your financial stability for yourself and your family.

#74: Get your priorities in order

What is more important to you?

Family, Work (vocation), Officiating (avocation), or playing golf (hobby)?

Remember that life is a balance. You're physical, mental, and emotional stability is important. Making sure that you can pay your rent or mortgage is important. Spending time with your family is important.

You have to make some hard decisions when it comes to putting your priorities in order. And it's different for everyone, so don't expect someone to hand you the answer.

#75: *Communicate and be honest*

Step 1: Establish how you're going to communicate

Do calendars work for you and your significant other? Can you remember things without it being written down?

Whether you text each other, have a calendar on the wall at home, or use an online shared calendar, you need to decide the most efficient way to communicate your schedule with your family.

If you don't establish a means of consistent communication, you can expect frequent disagreements and disappointments.

Step 2: Establish expectations

Are you going to work basketball games 4 nights a week? Are you going to work every weekend basketball tournament May to August?

Establish the expectations you have and what expectations your family has on your schedule. This includes time driving to and from games, how many games you work per week, and how often you'll spend studying (watching film, reading all the books, and going to meetings).

Step 3: Communicate early and often

As soon as you get your schedule, you have to communicate it to your family. If there is a family conflict that you weren't aware of, and you can't miss it, then you have plenty of time to "turn back" the game without ruffling any feathers. Or even better, if your family has communicated an activity that you can't miss, you have time to block it before you even get assigned a game.

Don't wait to tell your significant other until the night before that you have a game; they may have planned on doing something with you. In this situation, no matter what you do, you're going to disappoint someone, whether it is your assigner and partners or your significant other.

#76: Plan time with your family

Once you have your priorities in order (no matter what order they're in), you need to set aside some amount of time with your family. Whether it's two hours to watch a movie once a week or two days at a vacation home, you need to have time with your family. Plan this time just like you plan your basketball schedule.

#77: *When you're at home, be at home*

Being at home with your family is always special. When you get a night off, don't spend time on your phone checking texts and answering calls: be present and put your devices away.

If you want to spend time looking at film from your games or studying the rulebook, make sure they know when you're doing it, but at some point you need to put it down and just be with the ones you love.

Working your "Day Job"

#78: *Communicate with your boss*

No matter what job you have or what your career is, it is important to communicate with your boss. If you have a job that sometimes conflicts with officiating, tell your boss and try to work with them to find a balance.

#79: *Plan ahead*

In most jobs, you can't take days off whenever you want to on short notice: can you say "pink slip"? Ask your employer for schedules of work events and your day-to-day work hours if possible.

If it is an hourly job, try to ask for some consistency. Then you'll be able to schedule games and still work your day job.

When you sit down to set your blocks for the season, have your work schedule, or at least a prediction of it using past schedules, to make sure you don't get a game while you're working.

#80: Be good at your "day job"

Step 1: Have your priorities in order

If you're just starting out and you're making $50 a game, you need to remember that your day job is the most important. If you've been officiating for 10 years and you have a game that might bring home $1,000, you need to weigh your priorities.

Step 2: Know your role

If it is your job to be told what to do: do what you're told and do it well. If your role is to supervise employees, then supervise them to the best of your abilities.

You need to make sure not to skimp on your job responsibilities just because you're in a position of power. Being irresponsible will make your standing at your day job a little rocky, so know your role at work.

Step 3: Work extra when you can

If you are constantly taking off early to work basketball games, then you risk alienating your co-workers and making your boss mad. No one likes an underachiever at work so don't be one.

Luckily basketball season is only a few months out of the year for most officials, so you have a long time to put in some extra time. When you get the opportunity to "overachieve," do extra work, or stay late, make sure you use that time to show your co-workers that you care about them and your job.

#81: Don't take advantage of your employer

There are going to be times when you need to ask your boss to get off early to make it to your game on time: don't take your boss's flexibility for granted.

If you ask off all the time and don't do your job well enough, you won't have that job for very long: rest assured that most officials can't make their game fees pay their bills.

Basketball Officiating

#82: Be professional

Step 1: Look the part

When you show up for a game, make sure you're dressed appropriately. During basketball season, you will need to show up to the game site in either business casual or business professional, depending on the level you're working. When you walk into the gym, this is the first impression that players, coaches, and administrators have of you, so make it count by looking put together.

When you're on the court, make sure you're well groomed (hair combed/tied up, facial hair groomed neatly) and that your uniform is clean and free of wrinkles.

Perception is almost half the battle when it comes to officiating, so if you look the part, you're well on your way to having a smooth game.

Step 2: Be on-time

Time is important. Your time is important: so is everyone else's.

When you show up late, you are implicitly saying that your time is more important that someone else's: that's not okay.

Being on time shows consistency and sets you up to fulfill all stakeholder's expectations of you as an official.

Step 3: Be courteous

When you're nice to people, you'd be surprised how they treat you: well... nicely.

In today's world, everyone needs a pick-me-up, and showing someone common courtesy when you walk into the gym makes the world that much more fun to live in. Sometimes people don't expect courtesy, so by being courteous you can exceed expectations.

Step 4: Follow through

When you say you're going to do something, do it. If you accept a game, there are a lot of expectations that go with it: being on-time, contacting your partners, contacting game administrators if needed, fill out required reports, etc.

If you say you're going to work a game, or don't block a date off and get a game, then you need to follow through, unless of course there is something of importance that you can't avoid. When you follow through with your responsibilities, you're communicating that you are a professional and deserve respect.

#83: Set consistent blocks for days off

Step 1: Create a plan

Write down days of the week that you want to have off. Take into account family, work, and relaxation time: after-hours work events, volunteering at your church, your child's dance recital, your favorite show, your "lower-body" day for weight lifting, etc. Decide how often you want to block a certain day.

Step 2: Block the days well before the schedule comes out

Once you have your plan and have decided which days, and how often, to block, go onto your scheduling program and block them. The amount ahead of time assigners schedule varies greatly, so make sure to know what their expectation is for blocks.

Step 3: Stick to the plan

Once the season starts, you could forget why you blocked certain dates. If you blocked a day that wasn't a major family event or a work obligation, then you may be tempted to remove the block and schedule a game. Next thing you know, you have 6 games in a row and realize the block was so you could have an off day.

#84: Prepare for the mental grind during the season

Officiating can be a mental grind. There are bound to be days when you're spent physically, mentally, and emotionally. Use some self-care strategies to help you through the rough days:

- Meditation: Using a set time of the day to meditate can do a lot for your peace of mind. You would be surprised how refreshed you feel after a quick 10 minute meditation session.
- Rest, Rest, Rest: It cannot be stated enough; rest can cure many different kinds of fatigue.

When you're working multiple nights a week and working a fulltime job, you're going to be tired. Use the down time you have to kick back and do something relaxing.

- Visit the Chiropractor: In some circles, they get a bad reputation, but ask any referee who works a bunch of games; they'll tell you that the benefits of a chiropractor know no bounds. Making sure your body is balanced can help you keep up with the grind of the season.

Enjoy Little Things: Binge watching your favorite show, going shopping, enjoying an adult beverage with co-workers, or playing with your dog can go a long way towards giving your mind the break you need to give your passion to officiating.

#85: Take advantage of the "off-season"

In this day and age, basketball is almost a year-round sport. Really the only time of year where there aren't any travel leagues or rec leagues playing outside of the season is August, and even then, you're sure to find some games to work.

When your main season ends, anywhere from February to April depending on what level you work, take some time away from officiating. There are always going to be games to work, but to continue being a great official, you need to rest your mind and body.

#86: Take care of your body

Step 1: Develop good eating habits

Apart from helping you stay fit for officiating, eating healthy is going to improve your overall quality of life. If you can create good habits like portion control, read nutrition labels, and stick to a calorie or macro count, you will see that it isn't so hard to eat healthier.

Eating and traveling can be a challenge. Once you have good habits established, try to make sure you stick to them once you're in season. Try to pack whatever food you can and stay away from eating fast food and convenience store food.

No one is saying you can't eat the good things like fried chicken, soda, and Oreos, but eating healthy most of the time allows you to indulge when you feel like it.

Step 2: Exercise

The same as eating habits can be said for exercise. You're not just preparing your body to run up and down a court: you are improving your health which is going to improve your longevity and overall quality of life.

Some officials do a 20 minute workout with a mix of cardio and light lifting every day. Some officials body build and work specific muscle groups 4-5 days a week. Some just get up and run 2 miles in the morning. Do what works for you and your goals, but the most important thing is just exercising in some form or fashion.

Step 3: Warm up

Most physical therapists and trainers will tell you that the warm-up is essential to peak physical performance and injury prevention. Some health professionals disagree with the type of warm up you should use, but they all agree that as long as you're warming up, you are doing right by your body.

There are two main types of warm-ups: static and dynamic. A static warm-up refers to your muscles being still. So traditional stretching is considered to be static. Dynamic means using movement to warm-up. Doing activities like "high knees," lunges, and leg-swings would be put into the dynamic category

Using some type of warm-up will ensure that you're ready to run from tip-off!

Step 4: Cool down

Health care professionals also agree on the fact that a cool down routine will prevent injury and help your body recover from vigorous activity. Static stretching or using a foam roller to help your muscles maintain their flexibility will make sure you're ready for the next game.

Step 5: Stick to your routines

Once you've established healthy habits, stick to them. There will be days where expediency might say, "don't worry about your cool down" or "go ahead and stop at the gas station on your way home." If you can resist these kind of urges and stick to your healthy habits, you'll be able to continue your passion for much longer than you think!

Chapter 7: It's all About the Journey

It was early December at the start of my 4th year of officiating. I just had three of my first varsity games and one D3 men's game. I had a high opinion of myself to say the least; I thought I had "arrived."

One of my mentors texted me on a Friday morning and asked if I was open that night; I told him yes (who would've thought a hot-shot like me had a night off as a 4th year official?). It was a cross-river rivalry with a packed house, lots of emotions, and two challenging coaches.

The play was an easy one: a simple drive to the basket with some minor contact on a pass—I anticipated the contact that wasn't there. My whistle barely made a peep because I tried to stop it, but it was too late. Above the noise my partner, and mentor, must've barely heard my whistle because he stopped play. I quickly reported my foul, didn't switch like I was supposed to, and put the ball back in play. Those coaches had me the rest of the game.

Officiating is an avocation of blood, sweat, and tears. I knew this. But I still wanted more, and I wanted it right then and there.

You'll hear many officials say "trust the process." The process means that when you work really hard and make significant improvement, you may not get the big game the end of that year; you'll probably have to wait until the next year or the year after that. It may seem unfair, but there's a process for a reason: my number 1 reason occurred to me on that Friday night game.

Needless to say, I started to "trust the process," and from that moment forward I knew officiating was a passion that I would never "master," but I knew it would be fun trying.

What does it take?

#88: Be in shape

If you want to be a successful official, you need to be in shape. Many times officials complain about injuries and chronic pains, but these can be avoided by staying in shape throughout the year, not just during basketball season.

Taking pride in your physical appearance and being able to run with players, who don't get older, will make you continue to love officiating. People will also look at you as someone who can be counted on with their effort on the court.

#89: Be self-aware

Knowing what goes on around you is vital, but what is even more important is knowing what you're doing at all times. If you take the time to be knowledgeable, you will catch yourself before you fall. Plus you won't have someone critiquing you every night on the court, so you need to be your own evaluator.

#90: *Be dedicated*

Anything in life worth your time deserves dedication. Ron Swanson has a great quote for this: "You can't half ass two things at once. Whole ass one thing at a time." You definitely need balance in your life, and no one expects you to make basketball the most important thing in your life, but anything worth doing deserves your upmost time and attention.

#91: *Be passionate*

Elation. Sadness. Excitement. Anxiety.

All of these emotions will be felt if you're a basketball official. Officiating is definitely a roller coaster, but no matter what, you have to be passionate to be successful. Give it your whole heart, and your passion will carry you a long way.

#92: *Be present*

For many officiating is the one time where they have a single focus at any given time. When you're "in the game," nothing else in the world matters during that specific time. Relish the opportunities to get lost in the game and forget that you are an adult with numerous responsibilities in the world.

#93: Be humble

Ego is definitely something that is necessary in every official, but being humble will ensure that you are respected when you walk on the court. Being able to admit that you're wrong shows a lot of character, and guess what: you're going to be wrong quite a bit, so it's better to just admit it when it happens.

#94: Be persistent

There will be plenty of bumps in the road on your officiating journey. The ability to keep going will signal whether you're cut out for it. Being persistent will give you the opportunity to advance and grow as a referee.

#95: Have the right people in your life

It doesn't matter what aspect of life you're in, you need three types of people in your life: cheerleaders, teachers, and someone to tell you like it is.

To sustain any endeavor, you have to have a support system that is encouraging you to move forward.

Cheerleaders will ensure that you keep moving forward, even if you're moving backwards.

As humans, we are always learning. We learn best when we have a mix of people that want to share experiences and wisdom. The teachers in your officiating life may be a fellow official that you started with, your supervisor, mentor, or spouse. Use them to learn and return the favor.

Sometimes we need a good kick in the butt. Many times in your officiating journey you're going to be wrong, and sometimes you won't know it unless you have a person who is willing to be honest with you. Whether it is a fellow official, friend, or spouse, use these people to grow from your mistakes.

Is it really that hard?

#96: Develop thick skin

You are going to love officiating. But sometimes people aren't going to love that you're officiating.

There seems to be this thought that people who wear stripes are out to get teams or are in it to see a certain team win.

If fans, coaches, and players spent 5 minutes listening to two great officials, who have a spectacular bond through officiating, they'd know that officials give their heart and soul to the game.

The greatest thing is that as an official, you have one of the best bonds of all: friendships that can walk through fire together. If you walk through a game with a fellow official and ignore the noise, you'll work every game like it's your last and take pride in doing something that not many people can do.

#97: Strive for the "perfect game"

Every official, regardless of which sport, will tell you that no one has ever worked a perfect game. This is definitely true, but that doesn't mean you can't try to be the first.

A wise official once said that everyone needs a "pie in the sky goal." Your pie in the sky should be the perfect game and here's why: even if you never achieve that perfect game, you will be an official that your peers will want to work with and you'll see guaranteed success.

#98: Laugh at the little moments

Step 1: Don't take yourself too seriously

Hopefully you've realized that you are not going to be perfect on the court (but still try...). Obviously there are times when you need to be serious to reflect your surroundings, but many times we can relax and show an emotion other than "stone cold." Take the opportunity to laugh a little, mostly at yourself. If you take a little stumble on the court, or any other "YouTube moment", don't be afraid to joke with a player, a coach, your partners, or even a fan. Officials should be known for their unfaltering emotions during tough situations, but there are still plenty of times to laugh at yourself.

Step 2: Look for the positives

In a game that is mentally and physically taxing, there are going to be plenty of negatives: fans yelling at you, you missed to calls in a row, your knee is hurting, games starting late, partners who are difficult to work with, etc. If you focus on those negatives, officiating isn't going to be your passion for long.

Instead look for the positives: a player that received a technical foul early in the game quietly apologized later in the game, you had a smooth game with little friction, you worked with a great partner tonight, or there was a hospitality room with free food after the game just to name a few. If you seriously can't find any positives then there is this one: you work up this morning and have the opportunity to officiate.

Step 3: Smile on the court

Whether it is during a timeout and you make faces at your partner across the court or you are in the center position and you flash a smile at the lead official to get their attention, try liven it up. Smiling and laughter are more powerful emotions than frowns and anger. Since smiling is free, take full advantage of it.

#99: Know when to call it quits

Step 1: When you don't get those "big games" anymore

When you were a young official, you were trying to get that cross-town rivalry game and earn respect from your fellow officials and coaches. Once you have worked that cross-town rivalry for 10 years, all of a sudden, you don't have it this year... or the next.

Not getting the "big games" anymore doesn't mean you are done officiating whatsoever. Ask yourself why you aren't getting that game. If the answer is you just aren't as good anymore or you made a mistake, then you still have plenty of good years left, and maybe you'll get that game back. If the answer is because the new crop of officials and "younger" officials are ready for that big game, this can be a sign that you are getting near your time to step away, but don't worry: you still have plenty of good years left!

Step 2: Ask a friend

Questioning yourself isn't any fun. Maybe you had a tough game, or maybe you've injured yourself. When you start questioning yourself, go to a fellow official that knows you well and that you respect.

Ask that official their opinion on your abilities as an official. This may seem easy, but when ego plays into it, this is almost impossible. If you can internalize the fact that you're imperfect, you'll be able to take your fellow officials' opinions and help you determine if it is time to walk off the floor.

Step 3: When your body hurts...

When you are in the prime of your season, working a bunch of games and getting the "big games," there are going to be times where you'll be sore; most of the time that soreness is going to be that night or next morning, but you recover just fine.

Things change when you're hurting during the game consistently. Officials are paid to keep up with kids who only get faster, so as you advance in age, it'll get tougher. When you can't give the effort it takes to get up and down the floor for the level you're at, it is probably time to starting think about retirement.

#100: Stay connected to the game

As a veteran official, you'll have experience that cannot be replicated by video or film study. Your wealth of wisdom is something that should be passed down to the next official. Whether you're mentoring brand new officials or trying to help great officials make it to the next level, your experiences are important and will help another official in their journey.

There are quite a few ways to stay connected with the game and continue share your wisdom:

- Mentor new officials
- Mentor officials trying to move up
- Work lower level recreation leagues

- Be an observer or evaluator for your local association or conference
- A last option: be a coach (really this wouldn't be so bad)

#101: Have fun

Whether you're officiating to stay connected with the game, be a better coach, make extra money, or to just do something that is hard, you are part of a special group. Officiating basketball is definitely not easy, but it is rewarding because you can take solace in this one fact: not everyone can do it, but you can.

Most people would say to really feel successful, you have to enjoy what you do. Hopefully you have a "day job" that you enjoy and can provide for you and your family. As far as officiating sports goes, most people do it as a side job, which makes having fun while you do it even more important.

Rest assured that the journey of basketball officiating will challenge you and also bring you joy. There aren't many jobs that are hard to do, pay fairly well, and allow you to exercise at the same time. To fully take advantage of officiating, have fun while it lasts.

Nothing is easy in life, but there are always positives. Officiating will always have fun times that go along with the tough times.

Comparing officiating to a roller coaster is too simplistic. There are definitely sudden drops and moments where you rise up and feel elated, but there are also moments where you have to back up, go sideways.

Following these tips will ensure that you're a successful referee, but if you truly read the tips, read "between" the tips, and keep looking forward, you will find that the up-down, backward-forward, sideways journey is one that you should enjoy. You'll be proud to say you're a basketball official.

About the Expert

Although he wouldn't be comfortable with the term "expert," Steven Michaluk is no slouch on the basketball court. With 6 years of on-court experience in high school and 2 years working college basketball, he has proved his worth and is continuing to climb. Steven currently works high school basketball in Virginia and NCAA women's basketball. Although this book is about his passion in officiating, he has a few others he could write books about: enjoying time with his wife and dog at home, teaching 5th grade, and playing golf.

HowExpert publishes quick 'how to' guides on all topics from A to Z by everyday experts. Visit HowExpert.com to learn more.

Recommended Resources

- <u>HowExpert.com</u> – Quick 'How To' Guides on All Topics from A to Z by Everyday Experts.
- <u>HowExpert.com/free</u> – Free HowExpert Email Newsletter.
- <u>HowExpert.com/books</u> – HowExpert Books
- <u>HowExpert.com/courses</u> – HowExpert Courses
- <u>HowExpert.com/clothing</u> – HowExpert Clothing
- <u>HowExpert.com/membership</u> – HowExpert Membership Site
- <u>HowExpert.com/affiliates</u> – HowExpert Affiliate Program
- <u>HowExpert.com/writers</u> – Write About Your #1 Passion/Knowledge/Expertise & Become a HowExpert Author.
- <u>HowExpert.com/resources</u> – Additional HowExpert Recommended Resources
- <u>YouTube.com/HowExpert</u> – Subscribe to HowExpert YouTube.
- <u>Instagram.com/HowExpert</u> – Follow HowExpert on Instagram.
- <u>Facebook.com/HowExpert</u> – Follow HowExpert on Facebook.